Non-Religious Fun

CW00847854

Philosophy and Poetry f

Compiled by Hugh Morrison

Montpelier Publishing
London
MMXIV

Published by Montpelier Publishing, London.
Printed by Amazon Createspace.
Set in Calibri 11pt.
This edition copyright © 2014. All rights reserved.

Readings

Seneca, from *Letter LIV*

I myself have for a long time tested death. When? you ask. Before I was born.

Death is non-existence, and I know already what that means. What was before me will happen again after me. If there is any suffering in this state, there must have been such suffering also in the past, before we entered the light of day.

As a matter of fact, however, we felt no discomfort then. And I ask you, would you not say that one was the greatest of fools who believed that a lamp was worse off when it was extinguished than before it was lighted?

We mortals also are lighted and extinguished; the period of suffering comes in between, but on either side there is a deep peace.

For, unless I am very much mistaken...we go astray in thinking that death only follows, when in reality it has both preceded us and will in turn follow us.

Whatever condition existed before our birth, is death. For what does it matter whether you do not begin at all, or whether you leave off, inasmuch as the result of both these states is non-existence?

They are not long

They are not long, the weeping and the laughter,
Love and desire and hate:
I think they have no portion in us after
We pass the gate.

They are not long, the days of wine and roses:
Out of a misty dream
Our path emerges for awhile, then closes
Within a dream.

Ernest Dowson

Marcus Aurelius, from *Meditations.*

Of an operation and of a purpose there is an ending, or of an action and of a purpose we say commonly, that it is at an end: from opinion also there is an absolute cessation, which is as it were the death of it. In all this there is no hurt. Apply this now to a man's age, as first, a child; then a youth, then a young man, then an old man; every change from one age to another is a kind of death. And all this while here no matter of grief yet.

Pass now unto that life first, that which thou livedst under thy grandfather, then under thy mother, then under thy father. And thus when through the whole course of thy life hitherto thou hast found and observed many alterations, many changes, many kinds of endings and cessations, put this question to thyself: What matter of grief or sorrow dost thou find in any of these? Or what doest thou suffer through any of these?

If in none of these, then neither in the ending and consummation of thy whole life, which is also but a cessation and change.

Music, when soft voices die

Music, when soft voices die,
Vibrates in the memory;
Odours, when sweet violets sicken,
Live within the sense they quicken.
Rose leaves, when the rose is dead,
Are heap'd for the belovèd's bed;
And so thy thoughts, when thou art gone,
Love itself shall slumber on.

Shelley

Epicurus, from *Letter to Menoeceus*

Accustom yourself to believe that death is nothing to us, for good and evil imply awareness, and death is the privation of all awareness; therefore a right understanding that death is nothing to us makes the mortality of life enjoyable, not by adding to life an unlimited time, but by taking away the yearning after immortality. For life has no terror; for those who thoroughly apprehend that there are no terrors for them in ceasing to live.

Foolish, therefore, is the person who says that he fears death, not because it will pain when it comes, but because it pains in the prospect. Whatever causes no annoyance when it is present, causes only a groundless pain in the expectation.

Death, therefore, the most awful of evils, is nothing to us, seeing that, when we are, death is not come, and, when death is come, we are not. It is nothing, then, either to the living or to the dead, for with the living it is not and the dead exist no longer.

But in the world, at one time people shun death as the greatest of all evils, and at another time choose it as a respite from the evils in life. The wise person does not deprecate life nor does he fear the cessation of life. The thought of life is no offence to him, nor is the cessation of life regarded as an evil.

And even as people choose of food not merely and simply the larger portion, but the more pleasant, so the wise seek to enjoy the time which is most pleasant and not merely that which is longest.

Remember

Remember me when I am gone away,
Gone far away into the silent land;
When you can no more hold me by the hand,
Nor I half turn to go, yet turning stay.
Remember me when no more day by day
You tell me of our future that you plann'd:
Only remember me; you understand
It will be late to counsel then or pray.
Yet if you should forget me for a while
And afterwards remember, do not grieve:
For if the darkness and corruption leave
A vestige of the thoughts that once I had,
Better by far you should forget and smile
Than that you should remember and be sad.

Christina Rossetti

Marcus Aurelius, from *Meditations*

There is nothing which doth not proceed from something; as also there is nothing that can be reduced unto mere nothing: so also is there some common beginning from whence my understanding hath proceeded.

As generation is, so also death, a secret of nature's wisdom: a mixture of elements, resolved into the same elements again, a thing surely which no man ought to be ashamed of: in a series of other fatal events and consequences, which a rational creature is subject unto, not improper or incongruous, nor contrary to the natural and proper constitution of man himself...

He that would not have such things to happen, is as he that would have the fig-tree grow without any sap or moisture.

If I should die

If I should die and leave you
Be not like the others, quick undone
Who keep long vigils by the silent dust and weep.
For my sake turn to life and smile
Nerving thy heart and trembling hand
To comfort weaker souls than thee.
Complete these unfinished tasks of mine
And I perchance may therein comfort thee.

Thomas Gray

Seneca, from *On the Shortness of Life*

The majority of mortals...complain bitterly of the spitefulness of Nature, because we are born for a brief span of life, because even this space that has been granted to us rushes by so speedily and so swiftly that all save a very few find life at an end just when they are getting ready to live.

Nor is it merely the common herd and the unthinking crowd that bemoan what is, as men deem it, an universal ill; the same feeling has called forth complaint also from men who were famous...

It is not that we have a short space of time, but that we waste much of it. Life is long enough, and it has been given in sufficiently generous measure to allow the accomplishment of the very greatest things if the whole of it is well invested.

But when it is squandered in luxury and carelessness, when it is devoted to no good end, forced at last by the ultimate necessity we perceive that it has passed away before we were aware that it was passing. So it is—the life we receive is not short, but we make it so, nor do we have any lack of it, but are wasteful of it.

Just as great and princely wealth is scattered in a moment when it comes into the hands of a bad owner, while wealth however limited, if it is entrusted to a good guardian, increases by use, so our life is amply long for him who orders it properly.

Why do we complain of Nature? She has shown herself kindly; life, if you know how to use it, is long.

Farewell

Farewell to thee! But not farewell
To all my fondest thoughts of thee;
Within my heart they still shall dwell
And they shall cheer and comfort me.
Life seems more sweet that thou didst live
And men more true thou wert one;
Nothing is lost that thou didst give,
Nothing destroyed that thou hast done.

Anne Bronte

Socrates, from *Plato's Apology*

Let us reflect in another way, and we shall see that there is great reason to hope that death is a good, for one of two things:—either death is a state of nothingness and utter unconsciousness, or, as men say, there is a change and migration of the soul from this world to another.

Now if you suppose that there is no consciousness, but a sleep like the sleep of him who is undisturbed even by the sight of dreams, death will be an unspeakable gain.

For if a person were to select the night in which his sleep was undisturbed even by dreams, and were to compare with this the other days and nights of his life, and then were to tell us how many days and nights he had passed in the course of his life better and more pleasantly than this one, I think that any man, I will not say a private man, but even the great king, will not find many such days or nights, when compared with the others.

Now if death is like this, I say that to die is gain; for eternity is then only a single night. But if death is the journey to another place, and there, as men say, all the dead are, what good, O my friends and judges, can be greater than this?

Happy the Man

Happy the man, and happy he alone,
He who can call today his own:
He who, secure within, can say,
Tomorrow do thy worst, for I have lived today.
Be fair or foul or rain or shine
The joys I have possessed, in spite of fate, are mine.
Not Heaven itself upon the past has power,
But what has been, has been, and I have had my hour.

John Dryden

Charles Dickens, from *Nicholas Nickleby*

It is an exquisite and beautiful thing in our nature, that, when the heart is touched and softened by some tranquil happiness or affectionate feeling, the memory of the dead comes over it most powerfully and irresistibly.

It would seem almost as though our better thoughts and sympathies were charms, in virtue of which the soul is enabled to hold some vague and mysterious intercourse with the spirits of those whom we loved in life.

Alas! how often and how long may these patient angels hover around us, watching for the spell which is so soon forgotten!

Away

I cannot say and I will not say
That she is dead, she is just away.
With a cheery smile and a wave of hand
She has wandered into an unknown land;
And left us dreaming how very fair
Its needs must be, since she lingers there.
And you-oh you, who the wildest yearn
From the old-time step and the glad return—
Think of her faring on, as dear
In the love of there, as the love of here
Think of her still the same way, I say;
She is not dead, she is just away.

James Whitcomb Riley

Edward Bulwer Lytton, from *Conversations with an Ambitious Student in Ill Health*

A death that is connected with love, unites us by a thousand remembrances to all who have mourned: it builds a bridge between the young and the old; it gives them in common the most touching of human sympathies; it steals from nature its glory and its exhilaration, not its tenderness.

And what perhaps is better than all, to mourn deeply for the death of another loosens from myself the petty desire for, and the animal adherence to life. We have gained the end of the philosopher, and view without shrinking the coffin and the pall.

Excerpt from Charles Sumner

Death takes us by surprise,
And stays our hurrying feet;
The great design unfinished lies,
Our lives are incomplete.
But in the dark unknown
Perfect their circles seem,
Even as a bridge's arch of stone
Is rounded in the stream.
Alike are life and death,
When life in death survives,
And the uninterrupted breath
Inspires a thousand lives.
Were a star quenched on high,
For ages would its light,
Still travelling downward from the sky,
Shine on our mortal sight.
So when a great man dies,
For years beyond our ken,
The light he leaves behind him lies
Upon the paths of men.

Henry Wadsworth Longfellow

Marcus Aurelius, from *Meditations*

Is any man so foolish as to fear change, to which all things that once were not owe their being?

And what is it, that is more pleasing and more familiar to the nature of the universe?

How couldst thou thyself use thy ordinary hot baths, should not the wood that heateth them first be changed?

How couldst thou receive any nourishment from those things that thou hast eaten, if they should not be changed?

Can anything else almost (that is useful and profitable) be brought to pass without change?

How then dost not thou perceive, that for thee also, by death, to come to change, is a thing of the very same nature, and as necessary for the nature of the universe?

Excerpt from Ode on Intimations of Immortality

What though the radiance which was once so bright
Be now for ever taken from my sight,
Though nothing can bring back the hour Of splendour in the grass,
of glory in the flower;
We will grieve not, rather find
Strength in what remains behind;
In the primal sympathy
Which having been must ever be;
In the soothing thoughts that spring
Out of human suffering;
In the faith that looks through death,
In years that bring the philosophic mind.

William Wordsworth

Thomas Paine, from *The Age of Reason*

The consciousness of existence is the only conceivable idea we have of another life, and the continuance of that consciousness is immortality. The consciousness of existence, of the knowing that we exist, is not necessarily confined to the same form, nor to the same matter, even in this life. We have not in all cases the same form, nor in any case the same matter that composed our bodies twenty or thirty years ago; and yet we are conscious of being the same persons.

That the consciousness of existence is not dependent on the same form or the same matter is demonstrated to our senses in the works of the creation, as far as our senses are capable of receiving that demonstration. A very numerous part of the animal creation preaches to us, far better than Paul, the belief of a life hereafter. Their little life resembles an Earth and a heaven - a present and a future state, and comprises, if it may be so expressed, immortality in miniature.

The most beautiful parts of the creation to our eye are the winged insects, and they are not so originally. They acquire that form and that inimitable brilliancy by progressive changes. The slow and creeping caterpillar-worm of today passes in a few days to a torpid figure and a state resembling death; and in the next change comes forth in all the miniature magnificence of life, a splendid butterfly.

Departed comrade

Departed comrade! Thou, redeemed from pain
Shall sleep the sleep that kings desire in vain:
Not thine the sense of loss
But lo, for us the void
That never shall be filled again.
Not thine but ours the grief.
All pain is fled from thee.
And we are weeping in thy stead;
Tears for the mourners who are left behind
Peace everlasting for the quiet dead.

Lucretius

Marcus Aurelius, from *Meditations*

Thou must not in matter of death carry thyself scornfully, but as one that is well pleased with it, as being one of those things that nature hath appointed.

For what thou dost conceive of these, of a boy to become a young man, to wax old, to grow, to ripen, to get teeth, or a beard, or grey hairs to beget, to bear, or to be delivered; or what other action soever it be, that is natural unto man according to the several seasons of his life; such a thing is it also to he dissolved.

It is therefore the part of a wise man, in matter of death, not in any wise to carry himself either violently, or proudly but patiently to wait for it, as one of nature's operations.

My dearest dust

My dearest dust, could not thy hasty day
Afford thy drowsy patience leave to stay
One hour longer: so that we might either
Sit up or go to bed together?
But since thy finished labour hath possessed
Thy weary limbs with early rest,
Enjoy it sweetly: and thy widow bride
Shall soon repose her by thy slumbering side.
Whose business, now, is only to prepare
My nightly dress and call to prayer:
Mine eyes wax heavy and the day grows cold.
Draw, draw the closed curtains: and make room:
My dear, my dearest dust; I come, I come.

Sir William Dyer

Francis Bacon, from *Essay on Death*

I have often thought upon death, and I find it the least of all evils. All that which is past is as a dream; and he that hopes or depends upon the future dreams while awake.

So much of our life as we have discovered is already dead; and all those hours which we share—even from the breasts of our mother until we return to our grandmother the earth—are part of our dying days; of which even this is one and those that succeed it are of the same nature, for we die daily. And as others have given place to us, so we must in the end give way to others.

I know many wise men, that fear to die; for the change is bitter, and flesh wishes to refuse to try it: besides the expectation brings terror, and that exceeds the evil.

But I do not believe that any man fears to be dead, but only the stroke of death: and such are my hopes, that if heaven be pleased, and nature renews my lease for just another twenty one, I, without asking longer days, shall be strong enough to acknowledge without mourning that I was conceived as a mortal.

A parting guest

What delightful guests are they
Life and Love!
Lingering I turn away,
This late hour, yet glad enough
They have not witheld from me
Their high hospitality.
So with face lit with delight
And all gratitude, I stay
Yet to press their hands and say,
'Thanks. So fine a time! Goodnight.'

James Whitcomb Riley

Arthur Schopenhauer, from *Immortality: a dialogue*.

As far as you are an individual, death will be the end of you.

But your individuality is not your truest, innermost being: it is only the outward manifestation of it.

It is only the phenomenon presented in the form of time, therefore something with a beginning and an end.

But your true being knows neither time nor beginning nor end, nor the limits of any given individual.

It is everywhere present in every individual. No individual can exist apart from it.

So when death comes, on the one hand you are annihilated as an individual; on the other, you are and remain everything.

When I am dead, my dearest

When I am dead, my dearest,
Sing no sad songs for me;
Plant thou no roses at my head,
Nor shady cypress tree:
Be the green grass above me
With showers and dewdrops wet;
And if thou wilt, remember,
And if thou wilt, forget.
I shall not see the shadows,
I shall not feel the rain;
I shall not hear the nightingale
Sing on, as if in pain:
And dreaming through the twilight
That doth not rise nor set,
Haply I may remember,
And haply may forget.

Christina Rossetti

Marcus Aurelius, from *Meditations*

Up and down, from one age to another, go the ordinary things of the world; being still the same.

And either of everything in particular before it come to pass, the mind of the universe doth consider with itself and deliberate: and if so, then submit for shame unto the determination of such an excellent understanding: or once for all it did resolve upon all things in general; and since that whatsoever happens, happens by a necessary consequence, and all things indivisibly in a manner and inseparably hold one of another.

In sum, either there is a God, and then all is well; or if all things go by chance and fortune, yet mayest thou use thine own providence in those things that concern thee properly; and then art thou well.

Requiem

Under the wide and starry sky,
Dig the grave and let me lie.
Glad did I live and gladly die,
And I laid me down with a will.
This be the verse you grave for me:
Here he lies where he longed to be;
Home is the sailor, home from sea,
And the hunter home from the hill.

Robert Louis Stevenson

Peace, my heart

Peace, my heart, let the time for the parting be sweet.
Let it not be a death but completeness.
Let love melt into memory and pain into songs.
Let the flight through the sky end in the folding of the wings over the nest.
Let the last touch of your hands be gentle like the flower of the night.
Stand still, O Beautiful End, for a moment, and say your last words in silence.
I bow to you and hold up my lamp to light you on your way.

Rabindranath Tagore

O man, do not be afraid of death

O man, do not be afraid of death at all. Thou art immortal.

Death is not the opposite of life. It is only a phase of life.

Life flows on ceaselessly. The fruit perishes but the seed is full of life.

The seed dies but a huge tree grows out of the seed. The tree perishes, but it becomes coal which has rich life.

Water disappears but it becomes the invisible steam which contains the seed of new life.

The stone disappears but it becomes lime which is full of new life. The physical sheath only is thrown but life persists.

Sivananda Saraswati

Marcus Aurelius, from *Meditations*

...how absurd and ridiculous is it, ... as when one doth fall sick and dieth, to take on and wonder as though some strange thing had happened? ...whatsoever is dissolved, it is dissolved into those things, whereof it was compounded.

For every dissolution is either a mere dispersion, of the elements into those elements again whereof everything did consist, or a change, of that which is more solid into earth; and of that which is pure and subtile or spiritual, into air.

So that by this means nothing is lost, but all resumed again into those rational generative seeds of the universe; and this universe, either after a certain period of time to lie consumed by fire, or by continual changes to be renewed, and so for ever to endure.

The Vacant Chair

We will meet but we will miss him,
There will be his vacant chair;
We will linger to caress him
While we breathe our evening prayer;

When a year ago we gathered,
Joy was in his mild blue eye,
But a golden chord is severed,
And our hopes in ruin lie.

At our fireside, sad and lonely,
Often will the bosom swell
At remembrance of the story,
How our noble father fell;

How he strove to bear our banner
Through the thickest of the fight;
And uphold our country's honour,
In the strength of manhood's fight.

True, they tell us wreaths of glory
Ever more will deck his brow,
But this soothes the anguish only,
Sweeping o'er our heartstrings now.

Sleep today, Oh early fallen,
In thy green and narrow bed.
Dirges from the pine and cypress
Mingle with the tears we shed.

George F Root

Marcus Aurelius, from *Meditations*

Either all things by the providence of reason happen unto every particular, as a part of one general body; and then it is against reason that a part should complain of anything that happens for the good of the whole; or if, according to Epicurus, atoms be the cause of all things and that life be nothing else but an accidentary confusion of things, and death nothing else, but a mere dispersion and so of all other things: what dost thou trouble thyself for?

Goodnight

Goodnight; ensured release,
Imperishable peace,
Have these for yours,
While sea abides, and land,
And earth's foundations stand,
and heaven endures.
When earth's foundations flee,
nor sky nor land nor sea
At all is found
Content you, let them burn:
It is not your concern;
Sleep on, sleep sound.

A.E. Housman

Opening sentences

The life of the dead is placed in the memory of the living. **Cicero.**

Our dead are never dead to us, until we have forgotten them. **George Eliot.**

We shall be happy, for the dead are free. **Sara Teasdale.**

Death, therefore, the most awful of evils, is nothing to us, seeing that, when we are, death is not come, and, when death is come, we are not. **Epicurus.**

He that feareth death, either feareth that he shall have no sense at all, or that his senses will not be the same. Whereas, he should rather comfort himself, that either no sense at all, and so no sense of evil; or if any sense, then another life, and so no death properly. **Marcus Aurelius.**

As a well-spent day brings happy sleep, so a life well spent brings happy death. **Leonardo Da Vinci.**

Dying is a wild night, and a new road. **Emily Dickinson.**

Love has no age, no limit and no death. **John Galsworthy.**

Death is the veil which those who live call life; They sleep, and it is lifted. **Shelley.**

This life is worth living, we can say, since it is what we make it. **William James.**

The fear of death follows from the fear of life. A man who lives fully is prepared to die at any time. **Mark Twain.**

Death but supplies the oil for the inextinguishable lamp of life. **Samuel Taylor Coleridge.**

Death is the dropping of the flower that the fruit may swell. **Henry Ward Beecher.**

Death is a splendid thing - a warfare accomplished, a beginning all over again, a triumph. **George Bernard Shaw.**

No man can escape death; the only thing that he takes thought and care for is this, that what time he liveth, he may live as well and as virtuously as he can. **Marcus Aurelius.**

Then hath a man attained to the estate of perfection in his life and conversation, when he so spends every day, as if it were his last day: never hot and vehement in his affections, nor yet so cold and stupid as one that had no sense; and free from all manner of dissimulation. **Marcus Aurelius.**

If all be a mere confusion without any moderator, or governor, then hast thou reason to congratulate thyself; that in such a general flood of confusion thou thyself hast obtained a reasonable faculty, whereby thou mayest govern thine own life and actions. **Marcus Aurelius.**

If I must die
I will encounter darkness as a bride,
And hug it in mine arms.
Shakespeare.

What a small portion of vast and infinite eternity it is, that is allowed unto every one of us, and how soon it vanisheth into the general age of the world. **Marcus Aurelius.**

To die:—to sleep:
No more; and, by a sleep to say we end
The heart-ache and the thousand natural shocks
That flesh is heir to, 'tis a consummation
Devoutly to be wished.
Shakespeare.

I implore you to cherish my memory with joy rather than with sorrow. **Tacitus.**

Everything is changeable, everything appears and disappears there is no blissful peace until one passes beyond the agony of life and death. **Buddha.**

Sentences for committals and/or dispersals

...whatsoever was before to be seen, is by the continual succession of new heaps of sand cast up one upon another, soon hid and covered; so in this life, all former things by those which immediately succeed. **Marcus Aurelius.**

Let no man fear to die, we love to sleep all,
And death is but the sounder sleep.
Francis Beaumont.

Warm summer sun, shine kindly here;
Warm southern wind, blow softly here;
Green sod above, lie light, lie light -
Good-night, dear heart, good-night, good-night.
Mark Twain.

Death is not the monarch of the dead, but of the dying. The moment he obtains a conquest, he loses a subject. **Thomas Paine.**

And I will show that there is no imperfection in the present, and can be none in the future,
And I will show that whatever happens to anybody it may be turn'd to beautiful results,
And I will show that nothing can happen more beautiful than death.
Walt Whitman.

Look within; within is the fountain of all good. Such a fountain, where springing waters can never fail. **Marcus Aurelius**

Dear, beauteous death, the jewel of the just!
Shining nowhere but in the dark;
What mysteries do lie beyond thy dust,
Could man outlook that mark!
Henry Vaughan.

He has outsoared the shadow of our night; envy and calumny and hate and pain, and that unrest which men miscall delight, can touch him not and torture not again; from the contagion of the world's slow stain, he is secure. **Shelley.**

Nature hath its end as well in the end and final consummation of anything that is, as in the beginning and continuation of it. **Marcus Aurelius.**

I fall asleep in the full and certain hope
That my slumber shall not be broken;
And that though I be all-forgetting,
Yet shall I not be forgotten,
But continue that life in the thoughts and deeds
Of those I loved.
Samuel Butler.

Death is the certain end of all pain, and all capacity to suffer pain.
Johann G Fichte.

Death hath made his darkness beautiful with thee.
Alfred, Lord Tennyson.

To live in hearts we leave behind is not to die. **Thomas Campbell.**

It is by no means a fact that death is the worst of all evils; when it comes it is an alleviation to mortals who are worn out with sufferings. **Metastasio.**

Death is not grievous to me, for I shall lay aside my pains by death.
Ovid.

Death is the port where all may refuge find,
The end of labour, entry into rest;
Death hath the bounds of misery confined
Whose sanctuary shrouds affliction best.
The Earl of Stirling.

The long sleep of death closes our scars, and the short sleep of life our wounds. **John Paul Richter.**

The shadow of death is darkest in the valley, which men walk in easily, and is never felt at all on a steep place. **William Mountford.**

Death is the liberator of him whom freedom cannot release, the physician of him whom medicine cannot cure, and the comforter of him whom time cannot console. **Charles Caleb Colton.**

Death is a release from and an end of all pains: beyond it our sufferings cannot extend: it restores us to the peaceful rest in which we lay before we were born. **Seneca.**

After life's fitful fever, he sleeps well. **Shakespeare.**

He whom the gods love dies young, while he is in health, has his senses and his judgment sound. **Plautus.**

No evil is honourable: but death is honourable; therefore death is not evil. **Zeno of Elea.**

Like pilgrims to the appointed place we tend;
The world's an inn, and death the journey's end.
John Dryden.

As others have given place to us, so we must in the end give way to others. **Francis Bacon.**

All things that are in the world, are always in the estate of alteration. Thou also art in a perpetual change, yea and under corruption too, in some part: and so is the whole world. **Marcus Aurelius.**

Who knows that 'tis not life which we call death, and death our life on earth? **Euripedes.**

Sleep the sleep that knows not breaking,
Morn of toil, nor night of waking.
Sir Walter Scott.

Whenever his last day shall come, the wise man will not hesitate to go to meet death with steady step. **Seneca.**

Where is the subject that does not branch out into infinity? For every grain of sand is a mystery; so is every daisy in summer, and so

is every snow-flake in winter. Both upwards and downwards, and all around us, science and speculation pass into mystery at last. **William Mountford.**

Within a while the earth shall cover us all, and then she herself shall have her change. And then the course will be, from one period of eternity unto another, and so a perpetual eternity. **Marcus Aurelius.**

Whatever be my destiny afterward, I shall be glad to lie down with my fathers in honour. **Robert Louis Stevenson.**

Let these be the objects of thy ordinary meditation: to consider, what manner of men both for soul and body we ought to be, whensoever death shall surprise us: the shortness of this our mortal life: the immense vastness of the time that hath been before, and will be after us. **Marcus Aurelius.**

The way is not in the sky. The way is in the heart. **Buddha.**

For life and death are one, even as the river and the sea are one.
Khalil Gilbran.

Life's race well run,
Life's work well done,
Life's crown well won,
Now comes rest.
President Garfield's epitaph.

Also available from Montpelier Publishing:

The Simple Living Companion: Inspiration for a Happier and Less Stressful Life

'I have just three things to teach: simplicity, patience, compassion. These three are your greatest treasures...' (Lao Tzu, Chinese philosopher).

This anthology of quotations and passages on simple living from history's great writers and poets will provide inspiration and motivation on your journey to a simpler, happier life.

Non-Religious Wedding Readings: Poetry and Prose for Civil Marriage Ceremonies

Civil marriage ceremonies are increasingly popular, but it can be difficult to choose readings which are appropriate in a non-religious setting. A few well-known poems tend to appear regularly at civil ceremonies, but if you are looking for something different, this book could be the answer.

Non-Religious Wedding Readings contains a selection of 77 poems and prose passages on love and marriage from various writers dating from the seventeenth to the twentieth century. They retain the classic style of traditional church readings, but are entirely secular. In addition to celebrating married love, many of the readings also offer timeless wisdom for couples who are practical as well as romantic.

15249982R00032

Printed in Great Britain
by Amazon.co.uk, Ltd.,
Marston Gate.